"Still wie die Nacht."

"Still as the night." — "Comme la nuit."

Ancienne chanson d'amour.
Altdeutscher Liebesreim.

(Text Eigenthum der Verlagshandlung.)

English version by Mrs. John P. Morgan of New York.
Mrs. Morgan's translation is the only translation authorized by the Composer.

Adoptation rythmique française de L. de Casembroot.

Ruhig, aber nicht zu langsam.
Tranquille, mais pas trop lent.
Quietly but not too slow.

Carl Bohm, Op.326. № 27.

Still wie die Nacht, tief wie das
Still as the night, deep as the
Com - me la nuit, com me la

Meer, soll dei - ne Lie - - be sein!
sea, Should love, thy love ere be!
mer, Que ton a - mour soit grand!

F.H. 2785

Songs my mother taught me

Quand ma vieille mere

Als die alte Mutter

English words by *NATALIA MACFARREN*
French words by MADAME C.CHEVILLARD

Music by
ANTON DVOŘÁK
Op.55, No.4

Songs my mo - ther taught me

Quand ma vieil - le mè - re

Als die al - te Mut - ter

F.H. 2785

6

DEDICATION
(WIDMUNG)

(Original Key)

WOLFGANG MÜLLER (1816-1873)

ROBERT FRANZ, Op.14, No.1
(1815-1892)

BENDEMEER'S STREAM

Words by
THOMAS MOORE

Irish Air
Arranged by H. A. CHAMBERS

F. H. 2785

F. H. 2785

No, the ro - ses soon with - er'd that hung o'er the wave, But some blos - soms were gath - er'd while fresh - ly they shone, And the dew was dis - -till'd from their flow - ers that gave All the fra - grance of

To A.B.H.

I Love You Truly

Words and Music by
CARRIE JACOBS-BOND.

F.H. 2785

FLOW GENTLY, SWEET AFTON

ROBERT BURNS

J. E. SPILMAN

1. Flow gen - tly, sweet Af - ton, a -
2. How loft - y, sweet Af - ton, thy
3. Thy crys - tal stream, Af - ton, how

mong thy green braes, Flow gen - tly, I'll sing thee a song in thy
neigh - bor - ing hills, Far - mark'd with the cours - es of clear wind - ing
love - ly it glides, And winds by the cot where my Ma - ry re -

praise: **My Ma-ry's** a - sleep by thy mur - mur - ing stream; Flow
rills! There dai - ly I__ **wan** - der as noon ris - es high, My
sides; How wan - ton thy__ wa - ters her snow - y feet lave, As

gen - tly, sweet **Af** - ton, dis - turb not her dream. Thou stock - dove, whose
flocks and my **Ma** - ry's sweet cot in my eye. How plea - sant thy
gath - 'ring sweet flow - 'rets she stems thy clear wave. Flow gen - tly sweet

ech - o re - sounds through the glen, Ye__ wild whis - tling
banks and green val - leys be - low, Where wild in the
Af - ton, a - mong thy green braes, Flow gen - tly, sweet

Little Boy Blue.

Words by
EUGENE FIELD

Music by
ETHELBERT NEVIN.
Op. 12, Nº 4.

sol-dier was pass-ing fair;__ And that was the time when our lit-tle Boy Blue__

Kiss'd them, and put them there.__ "Now don't you go till I come!" he said, "And

don't you make an-y noise,"_____ So todd-ling off to his

trun-dle bed,__ He dreamt of the pret-ty toys._____ And

dolce

distinto ma *p*

wait-ing the touch of the lit-tle hand,— The smile of a lit-tle face.— And they won-der as wait-ing these long years thro', In the dust of that lit-tle chair,— What has be-come of our lit-tle Boy Blue, Since he kiss'd them, and put them there.—

dolciss.

p

p

„Ich liebe dich"
"I love thee"

Edvard Grieg

Ich lie - be dich wie nichts auf die - ser Er - den, ich lie - be dich, ich
I love thee more than an - y earth-ly crea-ture, I love thee,dear, I

lie - be dich, ich lie - be dich in Zeit und E - wig-keit! Ich
love thee, dear, I love thee now and for e - ter - ni - ty! I

lie - be dich in Zeit und E - wig-keit!
love thee now and for e - ter - ni - ty!

Ich den - ke dein, kann stets nur dei - ner den - ken, nur dei-nem
One thought of thee all oth - er thought drives from me, Pledged to thy

CRADLE SONG
(WIEGENLIED)

KARL SIMROCK

(Original Key)

JOHANNES BRAHMS
Op. 49, № 4

With gentle motion

VOICE

PIANO

Gu - ten A - bend, gut' Nacht, Mit
Lul - la - by and good night! With

Ro - sen be - dacht, Mit Näg - lein be - steckt Schlüpf' un - ter die
ro - ses be - dight; Creep in - to thy bed, There pil - low thy

Deck'; Mor - gen früh, wenn Gott will, Wirst du wie - der ge -
head. If God will thou shalt wake, When the morn - ing doth

weckt, Mor - gen früh, wenn Gott will, Wirst du wie - der ge - weckt.
break, If God will thou shalt wake, When the morn - ing doth break.

F. H. 2785

Gu - ten A - bend, gut' Nacht, Von
Lul - la - by and good night, *Those*

Eng'- lein be - wacht, Die zei - gen im Traum Dir Christ-kind-lein's
blue eyes close tight, *Bright an - gels are near,* *So sleep with - out*

Baum; Schlaf' nun se - lig und süss, Schau' im Traum's Pa - ra -
fear, *They will guard thee from harm,* *With fair dream - land's sweet*

dies, Schlaf' nun se - lig und süss, Schau' im Traum's Pa - ra - dies.
charm, *They will guard thee from harm,* *With fair dream - land's sweet charm.*

STÄNDCHEN.
(Serenade.)

FRANZ SCHUBERT.

Moderato.

PIANO.

Thro' the leaves the night winds mov - ing Mur - mur low and sweet;
Lei - se fle - hen mei - ne Lie - der durch die Nacht zu dir;
Jus-qu'à toi mes chants, dans l'om - bre, mon - tent dou - ce - ment:

To - thy cham - ber win - dow rov - ing, Love hath led my feet.
in - den stil - len Hain her - nie - der, Lieb - chen, komm zu mir:
Tout se tait: la nuit est som - bre: viens près d'un a - mant!

Si - lent prayers of bliss - ful feel - ing Bind us, though a -
Flüs - ternd schlan - ke Wip - fel rau - schen in - des Mon - des
Va, l'a - mour et le mys - tè - re veil - le - ront sur

part,
Licht,
nous,

Bind us, though a - part.
in__ des Mon - des Licht,
veil - le - ront sur nous,

On the breath of mu - sic steal - ing
des Ver - rä - thers feind - lich Lau - schen,
Ne crains pas l'œil té - mé - rai - re

To__ thy dream - ing heart,
fürch - te, Hol - de, nicht,
d'un ty - ran ja - loux,

To__ thy dream - ing heart.
fürch - te, Hol - de, nicht.
d'un ty - ran ja - loux.

Hear the night-in - gale, so ten - der; Would her strain were thine!
Hörst die Nach-ti - gal-len schla-gen? ach! sie fle - hen dich.
Je__ suis là sous ta fe-nê - tre pal - pi - tant__ d'es - poir:

Ev-'ry note, la - ment-ing, ech - oes Some fond sigh of mine.
mit der Tö - ne süs-sen Kla - gen fle - hen sie für mich.
nul n'a pu me re-con-naî-tre, Dieu peut seul me voir!

Ah! she knows the lov-er's wish-es, Mourns when hopes de-part,
Sie ver-steh'n des Bu-sens Seh - nen, kön - nen Lie-bes-schmerz,
que lui seul soit no-tre gui-de, va,___ ras-su - re toi:

Mourns when hopes de-part; Mov-ing with her sil-v'ry ca - dence Ev-'ry droop-ing
ken - nen Lie-bes-schmerz, rüh-ren mit den Sil-ber-tö - nen je-des wei-che
va,___ ras-su - re toi. Il pu-nit l'a-mour per-fi - de qui tra-hit sa

heart, Ev-'ry droop-ing heart. Let thy pit-y then re-store me,
Herz, je-des wei-che Herz. Lass auch dir die Brust be-we-gen.
foi, qui tra-hit sa foi. C'est ton a-mant qui t'im-plo-re

NONE BUT THE LONELY HEART
(NUR WER DIE SEHNSUCHT KENNT)

(Composed in 1869)

JOHANN WOLFGANG von GOETHE (1749-1832)

(Original Key)

PIOTR ILYITCH TCHAÏKOVSKY, Op. 6, Nº 6
(1840-1893)

None but the lone-ly heart
Nur wer die Sehn - sucht kennt,

Can know my sad - ness;_____ A - lone, and
weiss, was ich lei - de!_____ Al - lein und

34

F.H.2785

Joy of Love
Plaisir d'amour

Giovanni Martini
(1741 - 1816)

I gave up all for cru-el Syl-via's love;
J'ai tout quit-té pour l'in-gra-te Sil-vi-e,

Too soon I find an-oth-er owns her heart. The
El-le me quit-te et prend un au-tre a-mant. *Plai-*

joy of love comes on-ly to de-part; Its
sir d'a-mour ne du-re qu'un mo-ment, *Cha-*

sor-rows bit-ter through a life-time prove.
grin d'a-mour du-re tou-te la vi-e.

F. H. 2785

"Long as the stream-let its waves may soft-ly pour, The
Tant que cet-te eau cou-le-ra dou-ce-ment Vers

mead-ow pass-ing on its joy-ous way,
ce ruis-seau qui bor-de la prai-ri-e,

My love shall be thine," would Syl-via soft-ly say.
Je t'ai-me-rai, me ré-pé-tait Sil-vi-e.

Still flows the stream, but Syl-via loves no more.
L'eau cou-le en-cor, el-le a chan-gé pour-tant.

ON WINGS OF SONG

(Heine)

Maid of Ganges

F. MENDELSSOHN

sin - ken un - ter dem Pal - men - baum, und Lieb' und Ru - he
geth - er, There by the palm - y streams, In love and peace for

trin - ken und träu - men se - li - gen Traum,_____ und
ev - er, And dream our hap - py dreams,_____ and

träu - men se - li - gen Traum, our
dream our hap - - py dreams, our

sel' - - - - - - gen Traum.____
hap - - - - - py dreams.____

Florian's Song

Chanson de Florian

B. Godard

Ah! s'il est dans vo - tre vil - la-
Ah! tell me if you ev - er meet

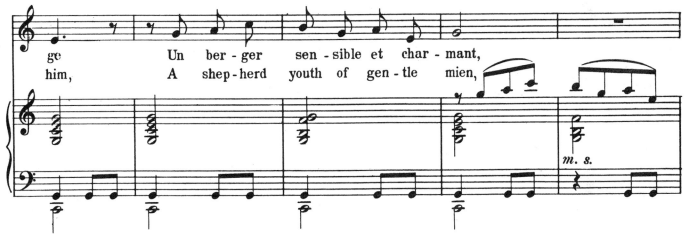

ge Un ber - ger sen - sible et char - mant,
him, A shep - herd youth of gen - tle mien,

Qu'on ché - risse au pre - mier mo - ment, Qu'on aime en - sui - te da - van-
One whom you love as soon as seen, One whom you love the more you

F. H. 2785

ta- -ge, C'est mon a - mi, ren - dez - le
greet him. Ah! he is mine, give him to

moi! J'ai son a - mour,___ il a ma foi.
me! His love have I,___ my faith has he.

Si par sa voix tendre et plain - ti-
If by his voice so sweet and ten - -

ve Il char - me l'é - cho de vos bois,
der He charms the ech - oes far and near,

Si les ac-cents de son haut-bois Ren-dent la ber-gè-re pen-
And if his flute-notes high and clear The tears of pen-sive hearts can

si-   -ve,   C'est en-cor lui,   ren-dez-le
ren-   -der,   Then is he mine,   give him to

moi!   J'ai son a-mour,___ il a ma foi.
me!   His love have I,___ my faith has he.

Si pas-sant pres de sa chau-miè-
When some poor soul his need con-fess-

„Ich grolle nicht"

"I judge thee not"

Poem by H. Heine

Robert Schumann. Op. 48, № 7

48

F.H. 2785

sah dich ja im Trau - me, und sah die Nacht in dei - nes Her - zens
saw thee, ay, I dreamt thee, And saw the dark - ness in thy heart - room

Rau - me, und sah die Schlang', die dir am Her - zen frisst,___ ich sah, mein
emp - ty, And saw the snake, that ev - er gnaws thine heart,___ I saw, my

Lieb, wie sehr du e - lend bist. Ich grol - le nicht, ich grol - le
love, how sore in need thou art. I judge thee not, I judge thee

nicht._____
not._____

F. H. 2785

STAR OF MY SOUL
(CARO MIO BEN)

TOMMASO GIORDANI
(1740 - 1816)

English version by
JAN L. LAWSON

Edited by
ALFRED MOFFAT

Thy Beaming Eyes

W. H. GARDNER

EDWARD Mac DOWELL, Op. 40, No. 3

54

„Du bist die Ruh'"

"Thou art repose"

Franz Schubert
Op. 59. No 3

Composed 1823

Langsam
Andante

Du bist die Ruh', der Frie - de
Thou art re - pose, Art peace - ful

mild, die Sehn - sucht du, und was sie stillt;
rest, Long - ing, that glows, Yet calms my breast;

ich wei - he dir,____ voll Lust und____ Schmerz, zur Woh - nung
I set a - part,____ With smile and____ tear, Thy dwell - ing

F. H. 2785

hier_____ mein Aug' und_ Herz,_____ mein Aug' und_ Herz._____
here:_____ Mine eye and_ heart,_____ mine eye and_ heart._____

pp

Kehr' ein bei mir, und schlie - sse du still hin - ter
En - ter thou in, And soft - ly close On all my

dir die Pfor - ten zu. Treib' an - dern Schmerz__
woes The door with - in. Let pain de - part,__

aus die - ser Brust, voll sei dies Herz___ von dei - ner_
And all_ an - noy, Full be my heart___ Of_ thine own

Lust,____ von dei - ner_ Lust.___
joy,____ of_ thine own_ joy.___

Dies Au - gen - zelt, von
May thy pure light My

dei - nem Glanz al - lein er - hellt,___
gaze con - trol, With ra - diance bright___

cresc.

f

F.H. 2785

o_ füll' es_ ganz,_ o_ füll' es_ ganz!_
Fill all_ my_ soul,_ fill all_ my_ soul!_

pp

Dies Au - gen - zelt, von dei - nem Glanz al -
May thy pure light My gaze con - trol, With

cresc.

lein er - hellt,_ o_ füll' es_ ganz,_
ra - diance bright_ Fill all_ my_ soul,_

pp

f

pp

o_ füll' es_ ganz!_
fill all_ my_ soul!_

'TIS THE LAST ROSE OF SUMMER
(QUI SOLA, VERGIN ROSA)

THOMAS MOORE

Air: The Groves of Blarney

1. 'Tis the last rose__ of__ sum - mer, Left__ bloom - ing a -
2. I'll not leave thee,__ thou__ lone one, To__ pine_____ on the
1. Qui__ so - la,__ ver - gin ro - sa, come__ puoi__ tu fio -

lone;__ All her love - ly__ com - pan - ions Are__ fad - ed and
stem;__ Since the love - ly__ are sleep-ing, Go,__ sleep__ thou with
rir?__ An - co - ra mez - zo a - sco - sa, e__ pres - so già a - mo -

✚ We give *C sharp* at this point, as popular tradition demands it; but unquestionably the note was *C natural* original-ly, according to theories in regard to the scale used in early Celtic music.

cay;___ And from love's shin-ing___ cir-cle The___ gems___ drop a-
din?___ Dal___ ven-to-tor-men-ta-ta In___ pre-da_a un rio des-

way!___ When true___ hearts lie with-er'd, And___ fond___ ones are
tin?___ Sul___ ce-spi-te tre-man-te Ti___ col-go, gio-vin

flown,___ Oh!___ who would in-hab-it This___ bleak___ world a-
fior!___ Su___ que-sto___ co-re_a-man-te co-si___ mor-rai d'a-

lone?
mor.

FAR FROM MY DEAR ONE
(LUNGI DAL CARO BENE)

GIUSEPPE SARTI
(1729–1802)

English version by
D. MILLAR CRAIG

Edited by
ALFRED MOFFAT

F.H. 2785

Far from my dear one part-ed,
Lun - gi dal ca - ro be - ne,
Life is but vain and joy - less;
Vi - ve - re non pos-s'i - o;

Pin - ing and hea - vy heart - ed,
So - no in un mar di pe - ne,
Far from my dear one part - ed,
Lun - gi dal ca - ro be - ne,

Drown-ed, drown - ed in tears I lie,
Sen - to, sen - to man - car mi il cor,

Drown-ed in tears I lie,
Sen - to man-car mi'l cor,
Drown-ed in tears I lie.
Sen - to man-car mi'l cor.

ROSE, SOFTLY BLOOMING

L. SPOHR
(1784 - 1859)

Edited by
ALFRED MOFFAT

F.H. 2785

Pride of my bo - som! I'll che - rish thee there,

Pride of my bo - som! I'll che - rish thee there.

Un poco più vivace

Smiles still are thine, ___ In de - cay's ___ wast - ing hour;

So, gen - tle flow - er, So gen - tle flow - er,

Sapphic Ode

Sapphische Ode   Strophes Saphiques

(Hans Schmidt)

English version by PAUL ENGLAND
French version by VICTOR WILDER

JOHANNES BRAHMS, Op. 94, No. 4

F.H. 2785

Thau_____ der mich näss____te.
Rain'd_____ on my fore___head.
Pleut_____ de la ro- sé____e.

Auch der Küs - se
Kiss - es sofi - ly
Mil - le fois plus

Duft mich wie nie be - rück__te,   die ich Nachts vom
culled from thy lips' red gar__land   Breath'd a dee - per
doux, quand la nuit est clo - se,   Est le frais bai -

F. H. 2785

"Who is Sylvia"
„Was ist Sylvia"

Franz Schubert

dor - ed   she   might   be, ___   That   a -
Al - les   un - ter - than, ___   dass   ihr

dor - ed   she   might   be.
Al - les   un - ter - than.

Is   she   kind, ___   as
Ist   sie   schön ___   und

pp

she   is   fair? ___   For   beau-ty   lives   with   kind - ness:
gut   da - zu? ___   Reiz   labt   wie   mil - de   Kind - heit;

To   her   eyes ___   love ___   doth   re -
Ih - rem   Aug' ___   eilt ___   A - mor

F.H.2785

74

F. H. 2785

Where'er you walk

GEORG FRIEDRICH HÄNDEL

to _____ a shade,

Where - 'er you walk, cool gales shall fan the glade;

pp

Trees where you sit shall crowd in - to a _ shade, _____

_____ Trees where you sit shall crowd _ in -

The Lost Chord

Adelaide A. Procter

Arthur Sullivan

F.H. 2785

what I was dream-ing then, But I struck one chord of mu-sic Like the

sound of a great A - men, like the sound of a great___ A -

men. It

flood-ed the crim-son twi-light Like the close of an an-gel's Psalm, And it

F. H. 2785

lay on my fe-ver'd spir - it With a touch of__ in-fin-ite calm; It

qui - et-ed pain and sor-row Like love o-ver-com-ing strife, It

seem'd the har - mo-nious e - cho From our dis-cord-ant life. It

link'd all per-plex-ed mean-ings, In-to one per - fect peace, And

„Du bist wie eine Blume"
(Heine)
"To me thou art a flower"

Anton Rubinstein

F.H. 2785

Mir ist, als ob ich die Hän - de auf's Haupt dir
Dear child, up - on thy fore - head My hands in

le - gen sollt', be - tend, dass Gott dich er - hal -
thought are placed, Pray - ing that God keep thee al -

te so rein und schön und hold, be - tend, dass
way So pure and fair and chaste, Pray - ing that

Gott dich er - hal - te so rein und schön
God keep thee al - way So pure and fair

und hold,
and chaste,

be - tend, dass Gott dich er - hal - te
Pray - ing that God keep thee al - way

so rein und schön und hold.
So pure and and fair and chaste.

Ein Schwan.

A Swan.

W. Henzen,

EDVARD GRIEG

F. H. 2785

zeit in die Run-de.
wa-ter-elf's pow-er,

Und doch bezwangst du zu-
Thou yet didst yield thee, My

letzt mich beim Schei-den mit trü-gen-den Ei-den, ja da,— da sangst du!
wait-ing re-ward-ed: What long thou hast guard-ed, Thy song, re-veal'd thee!

Du schlossest sin-gend die ir-di-sche Bahn doch, du starbst ver-
In rap-ture sing-ing Thou heav-en-ward wendest; On song up-

klin-gend: Du warst ein Schwan doch! ein Schwan doch!
wing-ing A swan thou end-est! thou end-est!

(Dr. Th. Baker.)

F.H. 2785

NINA
(TRE GIORNI SON CHE NINA)

G. B. PERGOLESI
(1710–1736)

English version by
D. MILLAR CRAIG

Edited by
ALFRED MOFFAT

F. H. 2785

THE SWEETEST STORY EVER TOLD

Words and Music by
R. M. STULTS

1. Oh, an_swer me a ques_tion, love, I pray,___ My heart for thee is pin_ing day by
2. Oh, tell me that your heart to me is true,___ Re _peat to me the sto_ry ev_ er

day;_____ Oh, an_swer me, my dear_est, an_swer true;_____
new;_____ Oh, take my hand in yours and tell me, dear,_____

rit.   *dim.*   *f a tempo*

Hold me close as you were wont to do._____ Whis-per once a-gain the
Is it joy to thee when I am near?_____ Whis-per o'er and o'er the

f   *p*

sto-ry old, The dear-est, sweet-est sto-ry ev-er told; Whis-per once a-gain the sto-ry
sto-ry old, The dear-est, sweet-est sto-ry ev-er told; Whis-per o'er and o'er the sto-ry

p   *rall.*

old,_____ The dear-est, sweet-est sto-ry ev-er told._____
old,_____ The dear-est. sweet-est sto-ry ev-er told._____

Tempo di Gavotte

Tell me, do you love me? Tell me soft_ly, sweet_ly, as of old!

Tell me that you love me, For that's the sweet_est sto_ry ev_er told.

Tell me, do you love me? Whis_per soft_ly, sweet_ly, as of old,

Tell me that you love me, For that's the sweet_est sto_ry ev_er told.

"Amarilli, mia bella.„
(Amarilli, my fair one.)
Madrigal.

Mezzo-Soprano or Baritone.

Giulio Caccini.
(1546-1614)

"Since first I met thee."

A. RUBINSTEIN.

Long years have wing'd their weary flight Since first I met thee, And tho' enshrined within my heart, I'd fain for-get thee; For as the clouds a-round the sun ob-scure its bright-ness, So thou hast robb'd my once glad

life of all its light - ness!

Oh, world so won-drous fair, Oh, heart, once free from care!

From out my in-most soul escapes a sigh:— From me now all hath flown,

That could in life a-tone For wea-ry hours of anguish long gone by.

AT PARTING.

SONG.

Words by
FREDERIC PETERSON, M. D.

Music by
JAMES H. ROGERS.

The sweet — est flow'r that blows,...............

I give you as we part...............

For you, it is a rose! For me it

F. H. 2785

is my heart! The

poco agitato.

fra - grance it............... ex - hales.................................

cresc assai.

f

poco dim. e rall.

Ah! if you on - - ly knew!.................................

colla parte.

Which but in dy - - ing fails

F. H. 2785

It is my love for you!

The sweet __ __ est flow'r that grows,.............................

I give you as we part.......................................

You think it but a

104

F.H.2785

To Maud Ulmer Jones.

WHEN SONG IS SWEET
Douce Mélodie

Music by
GERTRUDE SANS-SOUCI.

F.H. 2785

Spring hath man-y a rose to wear, kiss - ed of sun and
Car le Prin - temps est ve - nu A - vec ses ca-

dew, They are on - ly sweet my dear, When they bloom for
- resses, Et ses ro - ses sont pour toi Et ses belles pro-

you. Tempo I.
- messes.

Moon - light rays are bright - est dear when on you they beam,
Clair de lu - ne, cré - pus - cule, Beau sol - eil, aur - ore,

"When the Roses Bloom"

Louise Reichardt

Drink to me only with thine eyes

Arranged by HEALEY WILLAN

BEN JONSON
1573-1637

OLD ENGLISH AIR
Date uncertain

This Edition must not be performed in public without mention of the Arranger's name.

Copyright, 1928, by The Frederick Harris Co.

F.H. 2785

This song is also published in D♭ and G

thirst that from the soul doth rise, Doth ask a drink di - vine,

But might I of Jove's nec - tar sip, I would not change for

thine!

I sent thee late a ro - sy wreath, Not so much hon' - ring thee

As giv-ing it a hope_ that there_ It could_ not with - er'd be;_____ But thou there-on didst on - ly breathe And sent'st it back_to me;_____ Since when it grows, and smells, I swear, Not of_ it-self, but thee!

Early One Morning

Arranged by
HEALEY WILLAN

F. H. 2785

A Legend

Légende

(Poem by Pleshtchéyeff
after an English original)

P. Tschaikowsky, Op. 54, № 5
From the cycle, "Songs for Young People"

Child Je - sus in his gar - den
L'en - fant Jé - sus dans son jar -

fair Some sweet red ros - es once had grown,
din A - vait plan - té de bel - les roses.

He tend-ed them with lov-ing care, Think-ing to
Il les soi-gnait a - vec a - mour, Vou - lant s'en

make him-self a crown. A - las, some chil - dren
faire u - ne cou - ron - ne. Mais des en - fants du

from the vil-lage, Who one fine morn - ing came that
voi - si - na - ge É - tant ve - nus un beau ma -

way, Did Je - sus' ros - es put to pil - lage,
tin, Ont mis les ro - ses au pil - la - ge

And all the gar-den dis-ar-ray. "How now shall your___ poor
Et dé-vas-té tout le jar-din. «Pau-vre cou-ron-ne, com-

crown be made? They have not left a flow'r for you!"
ment la fai-re? Les beaux ro-siers n'ont plus de fleurs!»

"The thorns are left," Child Je-sus said,_____ "The thorns are left, and
«Mais les é-pi-nes sont res-té-es,___ ré-pond Jé-sus, ce-

they will do." So of the thorns a crown he
la suf-fit.» Puis, en cou-ron-ne les tres-

WEYLA'S SONG
(GESANG WEYLA'S)

EDUARD MÖRIKE (1804-1875)
Translated by Marie Boileau

HUGO WOLF

F.H.2785

To F.B.

JUST A-WEARYIN' FOR YOU.

Words by
FRANK STANTON.

Music by
CARRIE JACOBS-BOND.

1. Just a-wear-y-in' for you, All the time a-feel-in' blue,
3. Eve-nin' comes, I miss you more When the dark gloom's round the door,

Wish-in' for you, wonder-in' when You'll be com-in' home a-gain. Rest-less, dont know
Seems just like you or-ter be There to o-pen it for me. Latch goes tink-lin',

what to do, Just a-wear-y-in' for you.
thrills me through, Sets me wear-y-in' for you.

F.H.2785

LAST NIGHT.

(Christian Winther.)

English Words by
T. MARZIALS.

Music by
HALFDAN KJERULF.

day time, I dream of you by night, I
Mun de, und send' dir mei nen Blick, du

wake and would you were here, love, And tears............... are
schlugst mir die tief ste Wun de, nicht Ant wort

blind ing my sight. I hear a low breath in the lime tree, The
giebst du zu rück. Nur Seuf zer im nächt li chen Win de, vom

wind is float ing through,........... And oh! the night, my
Zweig ein Wink so fern,..................... nur küh ler Thau der

night the wood, The flow - ers that slum - ber so gent -
Gra - bes - nacht, zu leuch - ten - d'm Ster - nen ge - fun -

ly, The stars a - bove the blue,............... Oh!
kel, wo Lie - be ver - ge - het nicht............... trotz

heav'n it - self, my dar - ling, Is pray - ing, pray - ing for
Tod und schau - ri - gem Dun - kel, dich zu des Him - mels, des

you, for you.
Him - mels Licht. Tempo I.

F.H. 2785